Santa

Christmas Tree

Elf

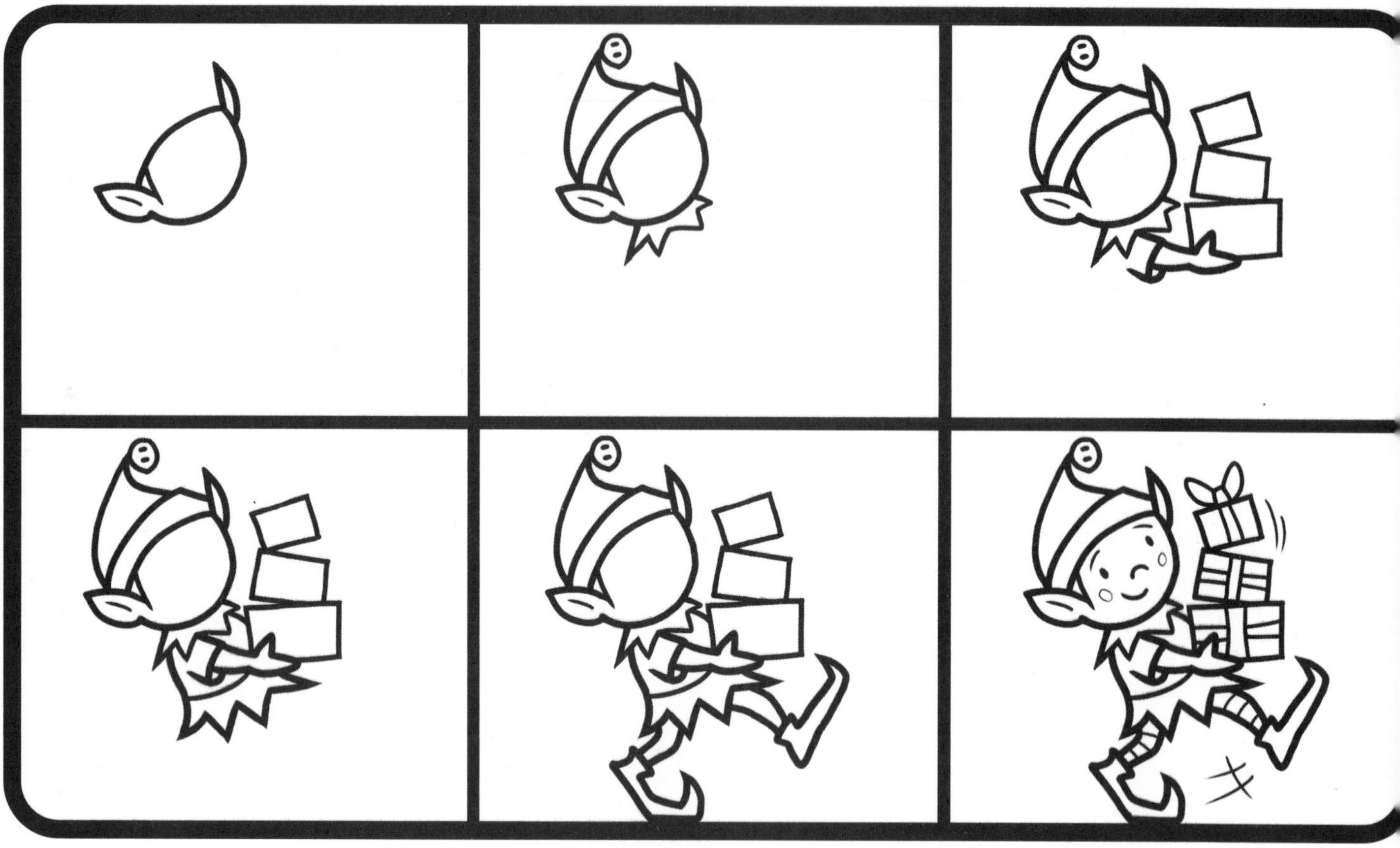

Stocking

Reindeer and Calf

Sledding

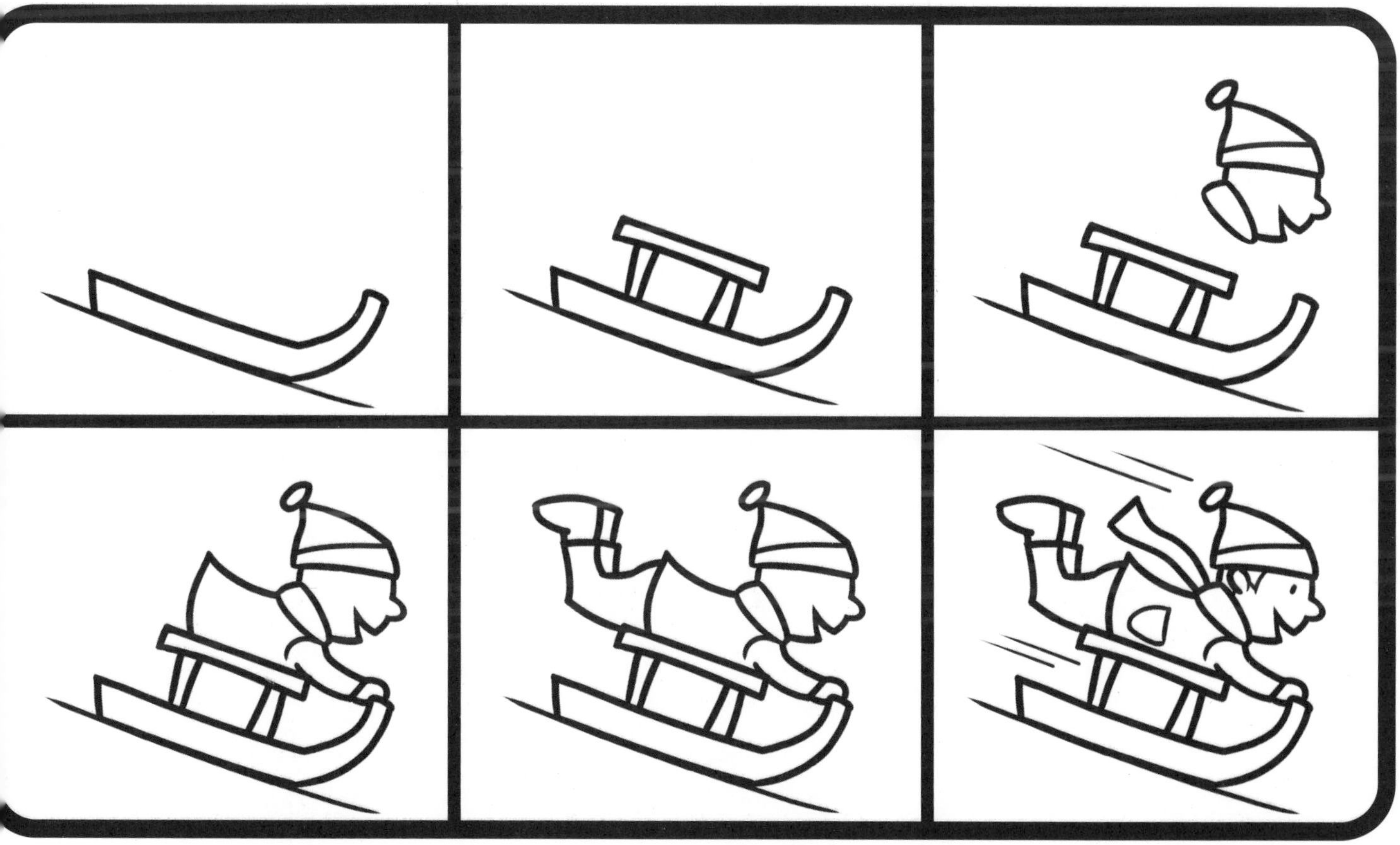

Snowman

Festive Penguin

Carol Singer

Christmas Wreath

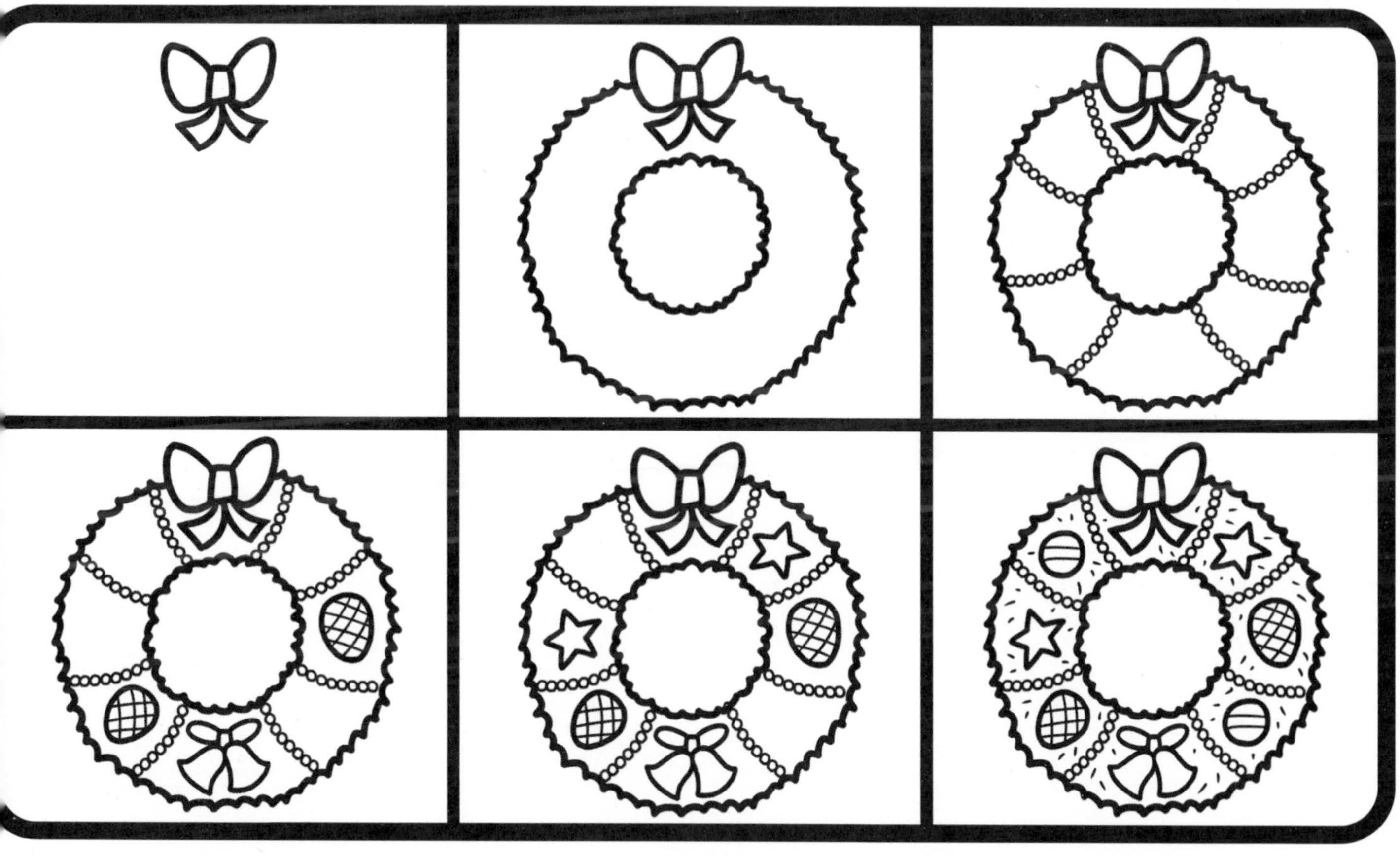

Christmas Fairy

Santa's Sleigh

Santa Coming Down the Chimney

Christmas Hearth

The Night Before Christmas

Family Christmas

Present Time

Christmas Toys—Dolly

Christmas Toys—Train Set

Excited Boy

Teddy Bear

Nutcracker

Sugarplum Fairy

Dreaming of Christmas

Elf Working

Christmas House

Snow Globe

Posting Christmas Cards

Robin

Christmas Shopper

Drinking Hot Cocoa

Christmas Market Stall

Christmas Tree on the Car

Christmas Clothes

Holly

Festive Polar Bear

Boy Wrapped Up

Making Snowballs

Building a Snowman

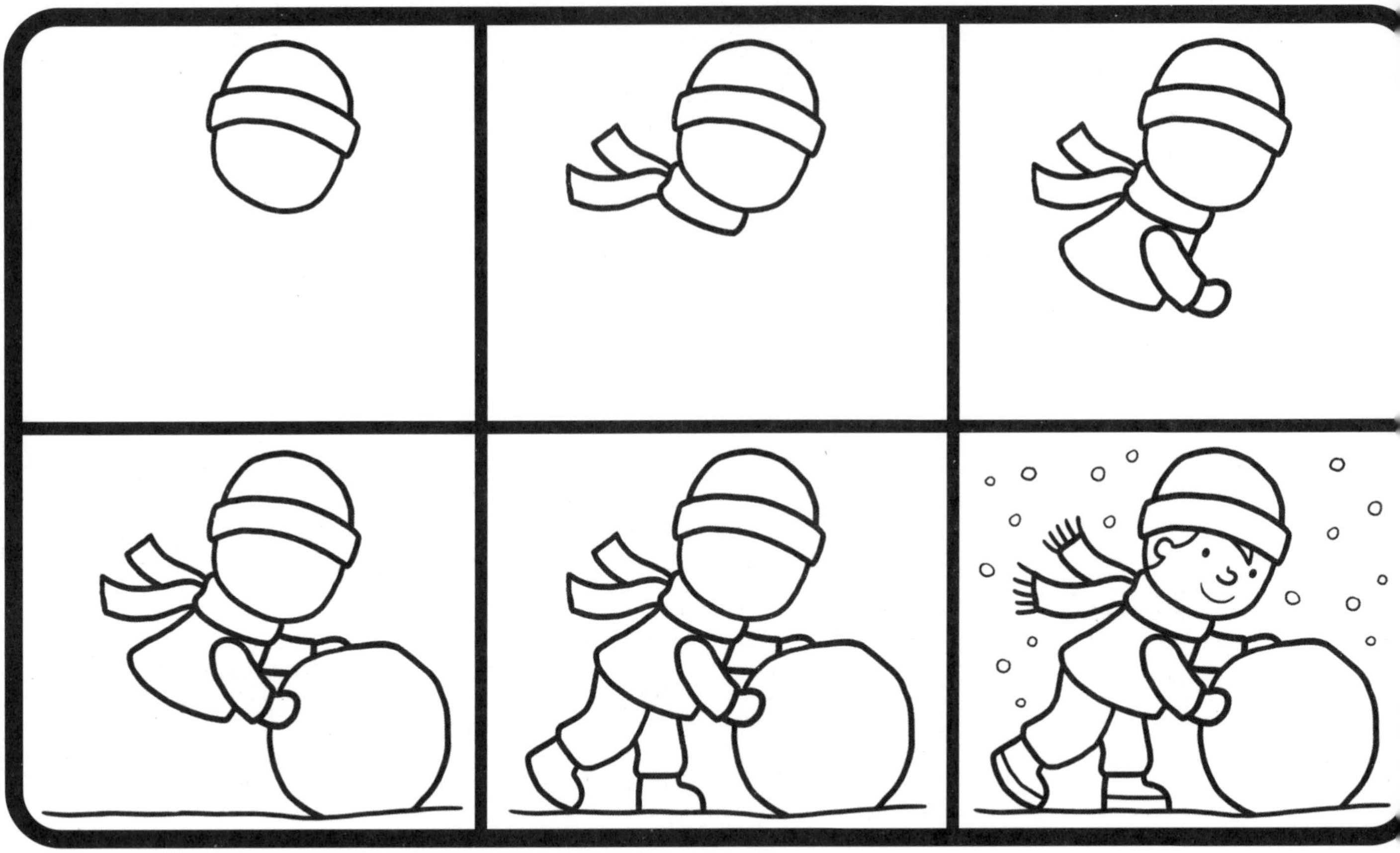

Snow Angel

Girl Wrapped Up

Santa and his Reindeer

Dasher

Dancer

Prancer

Vixen

Comet

Cupid

Donner

Blitzen

Mrs. Claus

The North Pole

Santa at the North Pole

Festive Dog

Christmas Store

Christmas Cupcakes

Deck the Halls

Christmas Dinner

Christmas Cracker

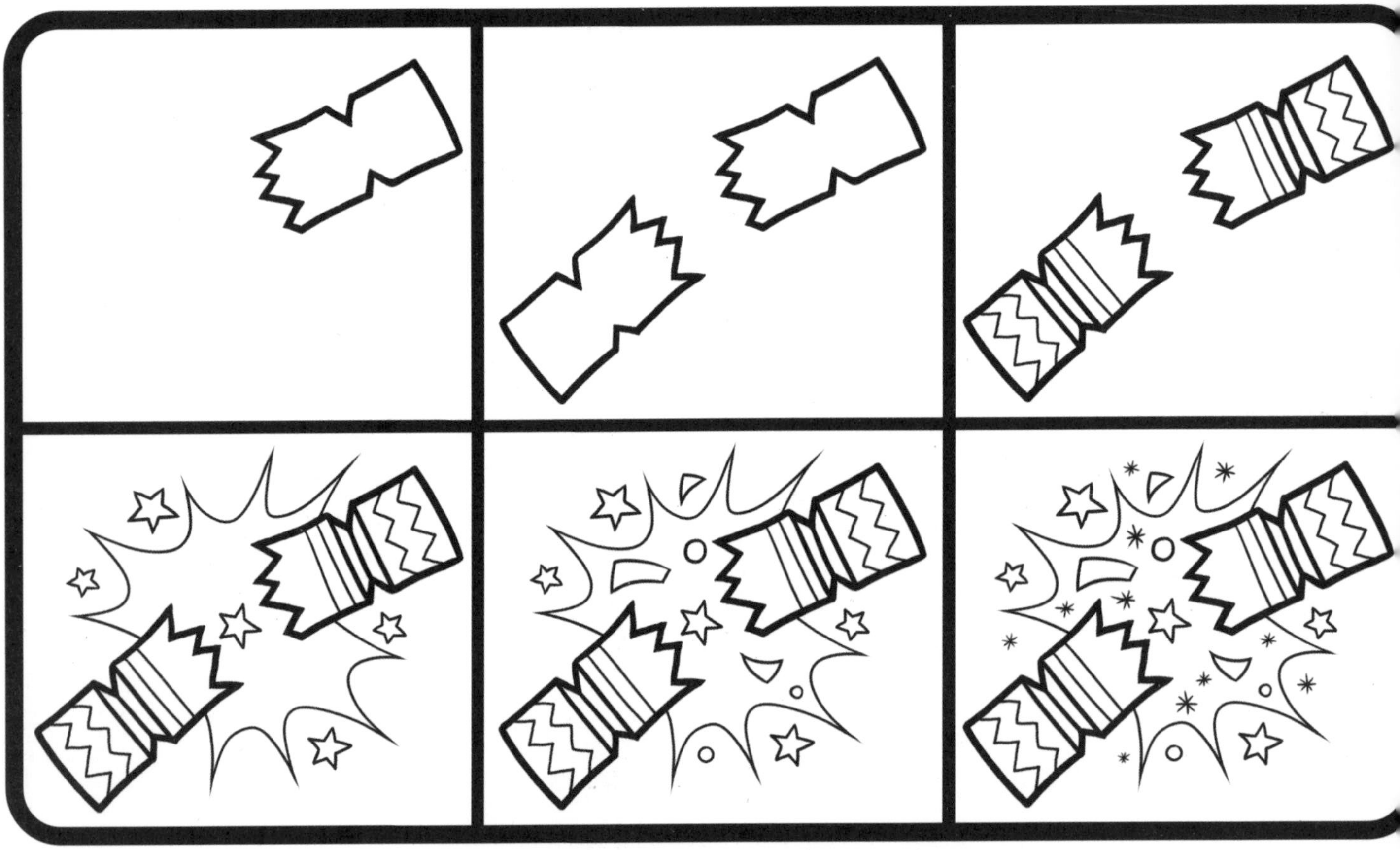

Grandpa Asleep

Gingerbread House

Ice-skating Friends

Pirouetting

Snowball Fight

Snow-woman

Snow-dog

Snowy Scene

Toasting Marshmallows

Christmas Choir

Angel

Driving Home for Christmas

Party Decorations

Party Time

Girl with Paper Crown

Party Scene

Boy with Paper crown

Mary

Joseph

Baby Jesus

Shepherd

Sheep

Donkey

Wise Man—Gaspar

Wise Man—Balthasar

Wise Man—Melchior

Camel

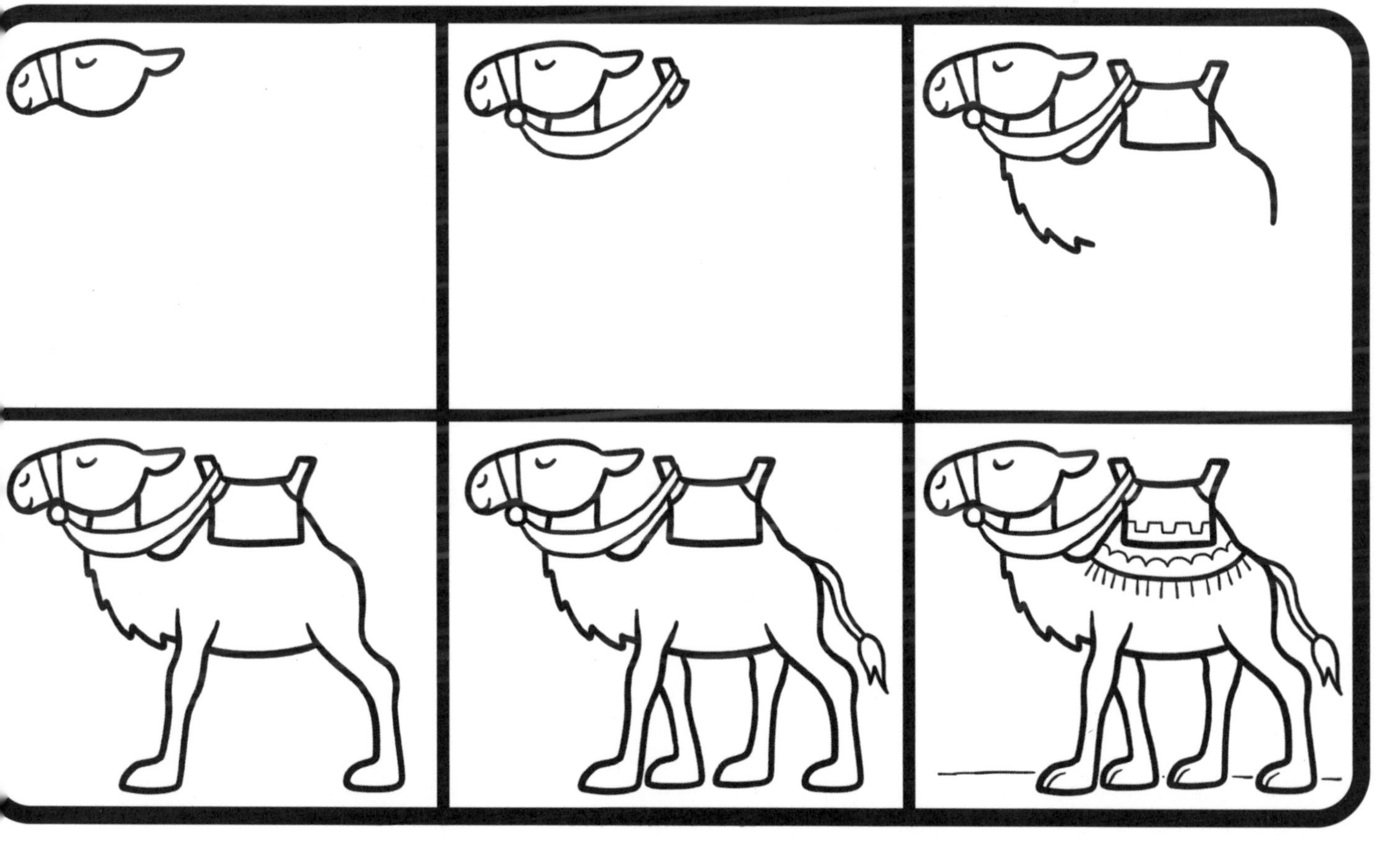

Jingle Bells

Gifts

Snowflake

ornaments

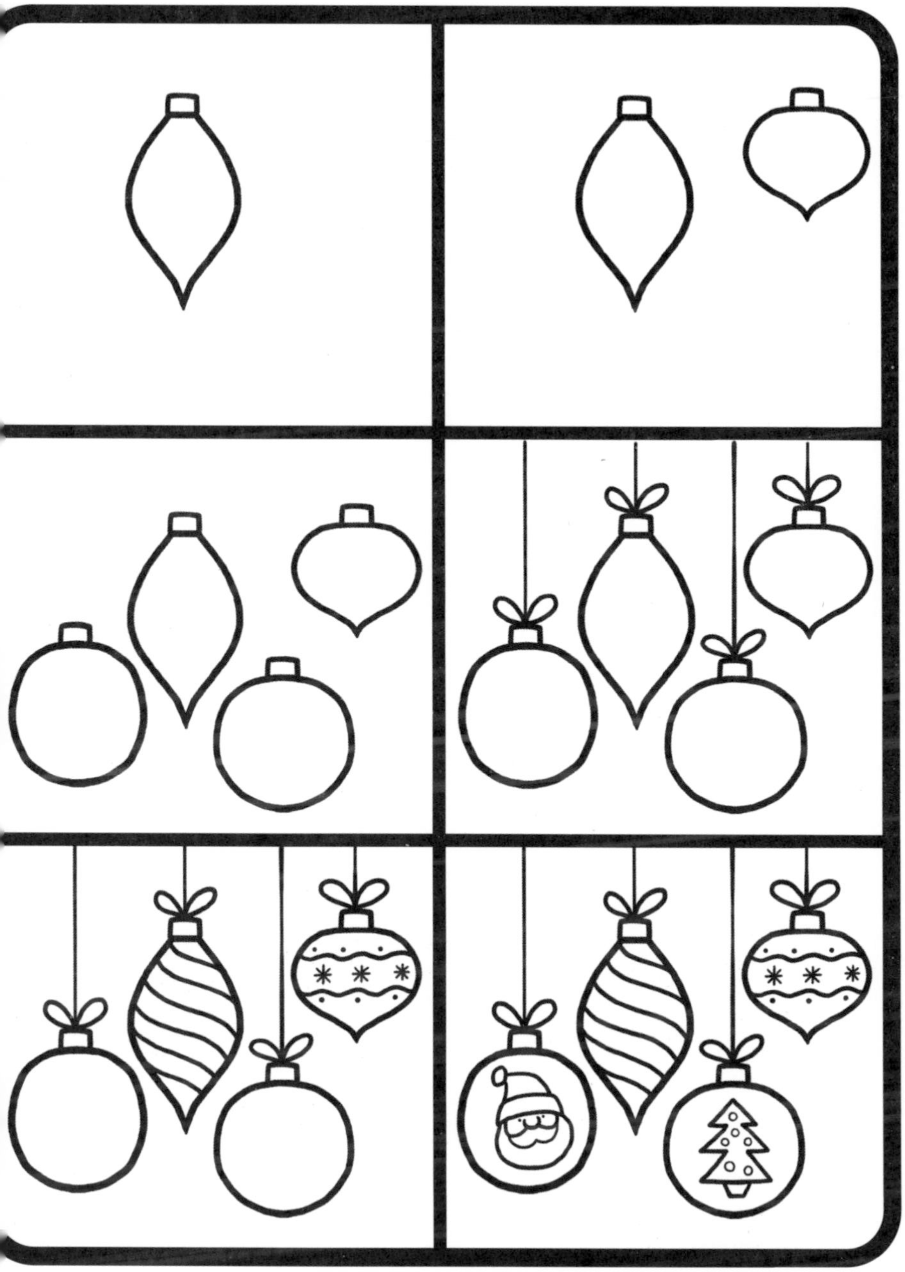

Candy Cane

Mistletoe

Poinsettia

Santa's Sack

Gingerbread Man

Drum

Roast Turkey

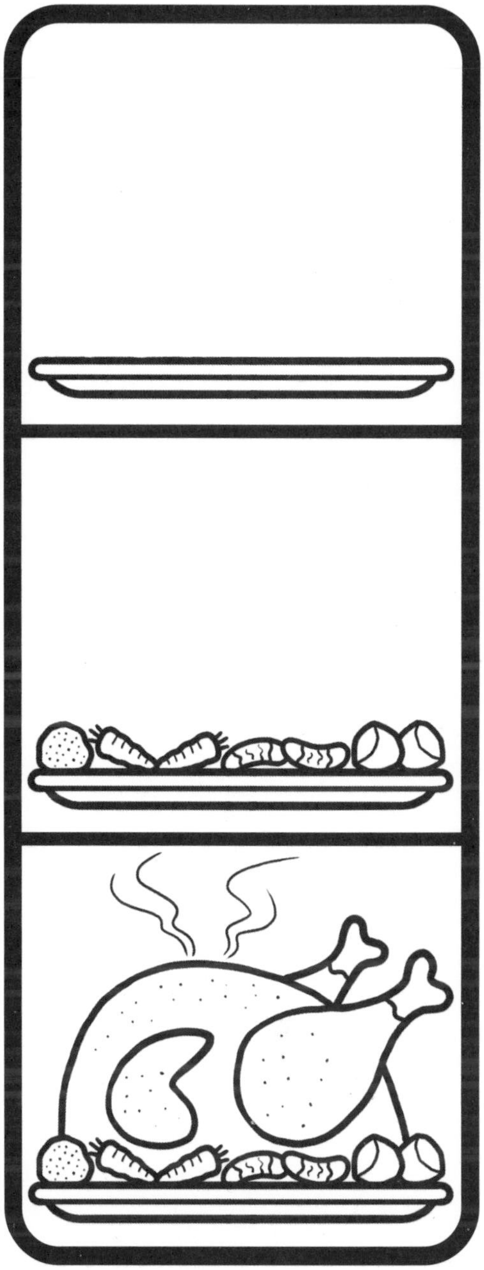

Christmas Pie

Dove

Christmas Candle

Party Popper